The Maine Christmas Song

Dedicated to the memory of my dear mother who spent her life helping young minds,
including mine, to expand, to think, and to act.
I would also like to recognize the town of Sidney, Maine, where I grew up,
and about which this song was written. — C. F.

To my three children, who spent their early years in Western Maine, and my
three grandchildren, who love it still. — C. B.

Manufactured by Regent Publishing Services Ltd Printed October 2021 in ShenZhen, China

First Edition

Hardcover ISBN: 978-1-954277-00-7
Ebook ISBN: 978-1-954277-01-4

McSea Books
Lincoln, Maine
www.McSeaBooks.com

Publisher's Cataloging-in-Publication Data
provided by Five Rainbows Cataloging Services

Names: Fullam, Con, author. | Baker, Cynthia, illustrator.
Title: The Maine Christmas song / Con Fullam ; Cynthia Baker, illustrator.
Description: Lincoln, ME : McSea Books, 2021. | Summary: Lyrics from Con Fullam's popular
"The Maine Christmas Song" matched with full color illustrations by Cynthia Baker.
Identifiers: LCCN 2021910024 (print) | ISBN 978-1-954277-00-7 (hardcover) |
ISBN 978-1-954277-01-4 (ebook)
Subjects: LCSH: Christmas music--Texts. | Christmas--Songs and music. | Songs. | Maine--Fiction. |
BISAC: JUVENILE FICTION / Holidays & Celebrations / Christmas & Advent. | JUVENILE FICTION /
Performing Arts / Music.
Classification: LCC PZ8.3.F85 Mai 2021 (print) | LCC PZ8.3.F85 (ebook) | DDC [Fic]--dc23.

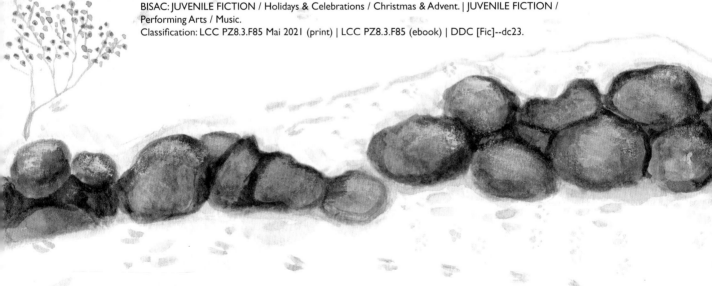

The Maine Christmas Song

by Con Fullam
illustrated by Cynthia Baker

There was a time when roads were
made of crushed rock and earth,

And the only tracks through the whitest of snow
    were those of footprints,
And pawprints, and hoofprints,
And the long straight lines of the sleigh.

It was a time when the gifts of Christmas
were made by loving hands,
And the holidays a holy time of giving
and sharing.

Neighbors with more gave to neighbors with less,
And the hopes of Heaven and peace on Earth
were shared by all.

ARTSY

TOY
DONATION

NEW!

ONLY

DROP PET
GIFTS
HERE

The Fir

Time has passed and much has changed,
But there is still a small corner of the earth
where old values have not been lost,

Where neighbors still share with
neighbors and children still believe
That to give is greater than to receive.

There's still meaning in the magic of Christmas
In the state where the Christmas trees grow,

Where neighbors still drop by
with cookies, breads, and pies
And warm themselves beside the
kitchen stove.

You can find a farmer hitching up his horses
To the sleigh that the family's had for years,

To give the children rides through
The snow-white countryside,
And the forests filled with timid whitetail deer.

Families still invite their friends and neighbors
In their search for the perfect Christmas tree,

Walking cross the frozen fields and rivers
Often times in snow above their knees.

It's the spirit of sharing, giving, and caring,
Hanging wreaths upon your neighbor's door.
That's the spirit of Maine at Christmastime—
From her mountains to her great Atlantic shore.

That's the spirit of Maine at Christmastime—
From her mountains to her great Atlantic shore.

The Maine Christmas Song

Con Fullam

There's still mean-ing in the mag-ic of

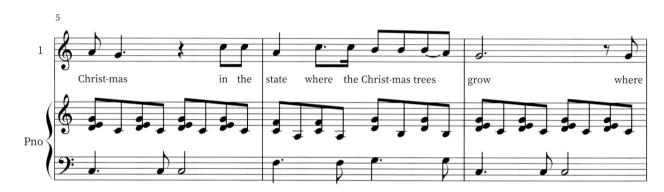

Christ-mas in the state where the Christ-mas trees grow where

neigh-bors still drop by with cook-ies breads and pies and warm them-selves be-side the kit-chen

stove   It's the | spi - rit of shar - ing | gi - ving and car - ing | hang-ing wreaths up-on - your neigh bors

door   That's the | spi - rit of Maine   at | Christ-mas time from her | moun-tains to her great At-lan-tic | shore

2. You can find a farmer hitching up his horses
   To the sleigh that the family's had for years
   To give the children rides
   Through the snow-white countryside
   And the forests filled with timid whitetail deer.

   CHORUS:
   It's the spirit of sharing, giving, and caring,
   Hanging wreaths upon your neighbor's door.
   That's the spirit of Maine at Christmastime
   From her mountains to her great Atlantic shore.

3. Families still invite their friends and neighbors
   In their search for the perfect Christmas tree
   Walking cross the frozen fields and rivers
   Often times in snow above their knees.

   CHORUS

Con Fullam is the composer and lyricist of "The Maine Christmas Song," which has sold over 100,000 copies since its original release. He is a multi-award-winning and five-time Emmy-nominated television producer, performer, publisher, writer, and recording artist; the creator and showrunner for the PBS series *Greenlight Maine*; and the executive producer of the award-winning PBS children's series, *Ribert and Robert's Wonderworld*, for which he co-wrote and co-produced the music. His movies about the fantastical characters The Wompkees, which he co-created, have aired on PBS and many other networks and are now distributed in 40 countries. He is the founder and director of Pihcintu, a multi-national chorus of 34 refugee girls from 22 countries, which has been featured by *The Today Show, Voice of America, National Public Radio*, and *Al Jazeera*.

Cynthia Baker is a multimedia artist working in clay and paint who has traveled and lived all over the world, but spends her summers in Western Maine. Her formal art training began when she was six years old during the occupation and reconstruction of Japan, and continued in Germany, Paris, Chicago, Maine, and Florida. She taught elementary art in Bridgton, where she painted the mural for the Maine Lakes Environmental Association. She designed sets for Maine Public Broadcasting's show *Franklin the Good Food Friend*, and painted panels for the original Magic Lantern Theater in Bridgton. She wrote and illustrated *A Moose Family Christmas, Four Seasons in Maine, Why Can't the Owl Sleep?* and *Cats and More.*

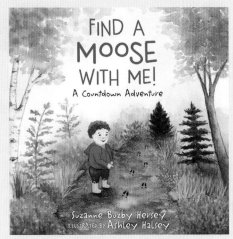

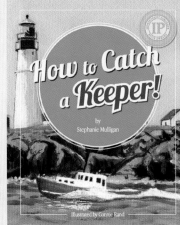

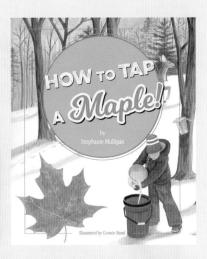

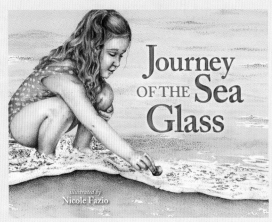

Find more great books on our Website!

McSea Books

www.McSeaBooks.com